CW01310039

A CHURCH NEAR YOU

by

DENIS DUNSTONE

The main entrance to most parish churches is through a south or north porch. Saffron Walden is unusual in using the west door as its principal entrance, in the manner normally confined to cathedrals and abbeys, and also most churches on the Continent.

A CHURCH NEAR YOU

During the confinement necessary to restrict the progress of the corona virus, one of the pleasures available was to creep away alone and sketch some of our neighbouring churches, in the spring sunshine. The result is a series of drawings which seek to emphasise the particular appeal of each of the subjects. I am not an architect, but I like old churches and I hope this little book might encourage its readers to go and have a look for themselves.

My personal favourite is the redundant St. John's in Duxford. Inside and out it is a gem.

Its richly chaotic exterior leads to a gallery of arched vistas inside. It is lovingly looked after by the Churches Conservation Trust.

Most of the churches within a half hour drive from Saffron Walden are constructed with flint and rubble. Stone was expensive and heavy to move unless you were near a waterway, while flint is hard-wearing and abundant in much of East Anglia. Brick was expensive but light, so useful if the ground was soft. It became more popular in the Tudor age.

Across England some 85% of medieval churches have a tower at the west end, then a nave and chancel with a square east end. This style is thought to have been Celtic in origin. Some 5% are cruciform with a central tower, like Ickleton and Thriplow. This is thought to have been influenced by Byzantine practice. They tend to be found in the south of England. Those like Duxford which are not cruciform but have a central tower are thought to have been Saxon, and are less common.

The apse was another continental creation. Originally there was an apse at both the west and east end of a church; and there are still examples of this in Germany. The apse was found widely in the Norman period, normally at the east end, but the Celtic style with the square east end prevailed. The only surviving west apse in England is at Langford near Maldon. The nearest east apse in Essex is at Pentlow near Clare. There are none in our area, though recent excavation in Wendens Ambo has revealed that Little Wenden church had one.

Not all cruciform churches were built as such. Berden is cruciform but has a west tower. It is in fact a traditional Celtic type which happens to have north and south transepts added at the eastern end of the nave.

Another English characteristic is the position of the main entrance. Reference is made earlier to the tendency to avoid use of the west door and to emphasise entry through a south or north door, often with a porch. Even odder is the fact that many churches do have a west door but seldom use it. One possible explanation is that with a single tower in which bells would have been hung, entry while ringing was taking place would have been inconvenient. In a cathedral with twin towers this problem would not have arisen.

This theory is undermined by the fact that even cruciform churches with a central tower tended to have a preference for north or south doors and minimised the use of the west door. It is further thrown in doubt by the fact that many churches had the ringing chamber one storey high. However the Camden Society changed this in the 19th century and insisted that ringers should be seen by the congregation and therefore be less likely to escape to the pub and avoid the service.

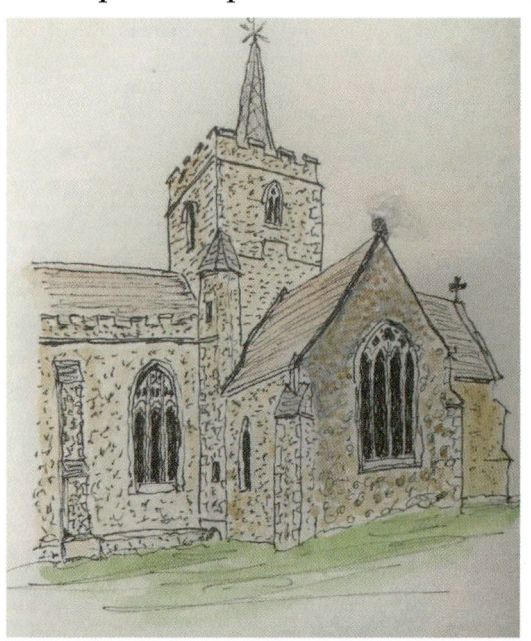

Thriplow is a perfect cruciform church with a west door, mainly entered through a south porch. It sits above the village and is a fine sight on the horizon.

There is in south Cambridgeshire a group of churches with central towers, cruciform at Thriplow and Ickleton, and without transepts as at Whittlesford and Duxford. In Essex, above the valley of the Wenden Brook there are two distinctive outsiders. At Littlebury Green the church is a kit-built export variety in corrugated iron developed for sending to missionaries in the Colonies. It is unexpectedly charming with interesting windows, while at Duddenhoe End............

Littlebury Green

.... the church is an attractively converted barn.

Ickleton is not only beautifully proportioned outside with a fine steeple; it is blessed with wall paintings, and arcades of Norman arches. Like many churches it has a small door in the chancel for the priest.

It is a characteristic of a majority of English churches that the main entrance is on the south side of the nave, sometimes with an elaborate porch. The side would normally have been determined by convenience, so it is interesting that in the majority of cases this turns out to have been the south side. Many churches had entrances on both sides, folklore suggesting that this enabled the devil to escape through the north door when a child was baptised.

At Wendens Ambo the north door was converted into a window in 1897. There is a west door which is little used. This is the former Great Wenden Church, Great and Little having been united in 1662. Ambo is Latin for 'both'.

Bartlow has the entrance on the north side. This church is notable for its round tower, a rarity in this area with only one other in Cambridgeshire and six in Essex, and said by some to be a way of avoiding corners where there was a scarcity of stone and a reliance on flint.

Little Abington, a typical Celtic arrangement ,with its Norman north door blocked up and tower stairway on the outside edge of the tower.

At Ashdon the south side contained the main entrance with its porch. This was because, until the Black Death in 1350, the village lay close to it. Clear evidence of this is the surviving Guildhall which stands just opposite the south door. After the Black Death, the village moved away and the south door was no longer used. It is now closed and the north door has become the main entrance. Consequently, this, the south side, with its unusual Lady Chapel is little seen and presents an unexpected sight to those with curiosity to explore.

Little Bardfield confounds the round tower argument. Its square Saxon tower built of flint has no masonry quoins yet the corners are perfect.

The plain north side of Whittlesford has remnants of a door and a small chapel in the chancel wall, and the tower stairway.

Chickney, half a mile up a farm track and set in deepest Essex, has a Saxon nave and pyramid tower, the pyramid being set outside the tower walls to allow drainage of rainwater. There is a small north door but the main entrance is on the south side. Chickney is in the care of the Churches Conservation Trust.

Alone in a perfect setting, high above the fields, Castle Camps is at first sight simply an example of a standard Celtic pattern: west tower, nave and chancel. However it has interest. It has an external tower stairway in a turret in the angle of a large buttress near the nave (compare Little Abington), and reveals a variety of materials in its construction. It is liberally buttressed and its north door has been very visibly filled in.

  Further north in Cambridgeshire is a church with buttressing that puts Castle Camps in the shade.........

.... Balsham is remarkable for the extent and variety of its tower buttresses. It is on well drained relatively high ground so the original construction must have been weak. Although these buttresses are an extra support and not part of the original idea, there is a certain attraction in seeing such evident examples of the management of forces.

From its commanding position, the tower of Elmdon church looks down on the village. It is a fine well-proportioned structure with a working clock, and forms an impressive focal point for the village.

In contrast the equally impressive Saxon tower at Strethall lies hidden between trees, deep in the countryside, down a farm track. This little church is fondly regarded and has the advantage of being full even when the congregation is small.

In the valley of the Cam close to the river, the railway and the Newmarket Road lies Little Chesterford. Its main street is a by-way and it is set in fields. Its church enjoys a peaceful and secluded position and has an unexpected charm. Unexpected because at first sight it is a long low plain building with a single roof line and few windows, and no tower. It is redeemed by its setting and its quiet modesty.

Further south, with its back to the main road, is the fine west end of Littlebury Church. With its striking porch, it relaxes among the trees of its churchyard, trying to ignore the roar of passing traffic.

By way of contrast Chrishall Church, up a narrow track and looking down across the valley of the Wenden Brook, stands almost deserted in the company of the former Rectory and a thatched cottage. The village moved north after the Black Death leaving this large church to peace and tranquillity. It has a long chancel and crenelations galore, and its interior is beautifully kept. It was recently given a new floor and seating and, with new catering facilities, it sets an example on how to sustain viability sympathetically when combining worship with other uses.

The view from the churchyard is of an unexpectedly hilly Essex.

It will be apparent by now that the tower of a church is a critical feature. It is in a sense the identifier of the church. The absence of a tower can be a massive handicap. Little Chesterford's belfry manages to make a sufficient statement, but Wimbish, which has lost two towers over the years, now has none at all. It needs one. Heydon lost its tower and north aisle to a Nazi bomb in 1940. The replacement is in dark brown brick with a sinister looking belfry and green pyramid roof.

Wimbish is an attractive and interesting church but looks bereft without a tower

It is the tower at Arkesden which makes the church. It stands high above the village and is a fine example of the best work of the Victorians. Heydon's modern tower is less successful.

The tower at Newport rides above the village and is a distinctive feature from some distance. The chancel is colourful with a variety of building materials

In England the earliest church towers tended to follow the line of Roman roads in the eastern part of the country. It is thought that they had various purposes: as a watch tower, as a prominent statement, and as a place for bells. The word 'belfry' incidentally has nothing to do with bells, but is derived from an old French word for a siege engine. Saxon and early Norman towers such as Strethall probably had low pyramid shaped roofs. These were either within the outer walls as at Berden and Rickling, or overlapping to carry rainwater away as at Little Chishill. The Normans brought a taste for bigger stouter towers. The spire of wood covered in lead was a sign of wealth. The tallest of these are in the eastern half of the country. The smallest example was called a Hertfordshire spike as at Wendens Ambo. Ickelton reveals how the pyramid shaped spire was extended upward, and Thaxted demonstrates the ultimate. The steeple is the combined tower and spire. From 1300 towers were often crenelated.

One of the features of the tower is its stairway for access to the top. Some like Arkesden have a turret made into an architectural feature, attached to the outside of the tower. Others have a more discrete and functional stairway inserted in the angle of the tower and the aisle or nave, as at Elsenham.

Essex was well wooded so some bell towers were built of wood as at Debden. There were also Roman bricks available from surviving remains. The tower at what was Great Wenden has bricks from a Roman villa. Later in the Tudor period brick was more widely used as at Ugley and at Meesden, just over the border in Hertfordshire.

Most medieval churches have one or two aisles. These became necessary when the population increased. This was seen at Wendens Ambo in the surviving church of Great Wenden, while Little Wenden had no aisles. This was typical in East Anglia where the enclosure of land came much later, and where there were a large number of small communities with their own small church. These remained without any aisles, as at Elsenham and Little Chesterford, or with a single aisle as at Whittlesford and Little Sampford. Some like Little Abington and Hadstock built a transept to accommodate memorials. Saffron Walden is an example of what typically occurred in East Anglia with large clerestory windows inserted in the walls of the nave, above the aisles built on either side.

From about 1300 it was fashionable to crenelate the walls of nave and aisles as at Chrishall, Chishill and Clavering.

Hadstock Church is full of character. With transepts and a large north porch it presents a complex picture. It has remnants of its Anglo-Saxon origins including the oldest door still in use in Britain. The church is in an ideal position in the village, being high up but also quite central. The south door faced away from the village and is now shut off.

Little Chishill, when approached from Walden, first appears as a silhouette among trees on the top of a hill. The distinctive pyramid tower stands out. Up a footpath through trees it suddenly appears, tranquil, amiable, well proportioned and with oddities to feast the eye of the curious. The churchyard, full of birdsong, remote and peaceful, has the untidiness of nature, cleverly balanced with respect for the location; the grass and bushes are under control, but not too much. Rather more than a short drive from Walden, it offers the most rewarding total experience, even if locked.

Great Chishill is perfectly proportioned. Like Chrishall and Clavering it is heavily crenellated. The battlements are purely decorative and served no military function. It stands in a pretty churchyard on the edge of the escarpment with a fine view over Cambridgeshire to the north. It is some distance from Little Chishill and quite different. It stands at the centre of the village and is a typical Essex church even though it now lies in Cambridgeshire.

Debden is unique due to the influence of an 18th century benefactor who liked pinnacles and created an octagonal chancel. Its tower is similar to that at Quendon, which is an exceptionally pretty little church.

Thaxted is in a class of its own and so full of worthy detail that a whole book could be devoted to it, but in the end it is the spire which is so awe-inspiring.

Some have elaborate porches as at Radwinter, while at Meesden the Elizabethan porch dominates the little church.

The north porch at Thaxted is a marvellous piece of art. Pevsner in his book 'The Englishness of English Art' argues that the preference for porches in England is due to a desire to compartmentalise and so create spaces such as chapels and transepts. They are certainly an English feature. Some had an upper chamber as here and at Radwinter; the uses varied from accommodation for the priest to a store-room or a useful space just to dump things.

Hempstead has a brick extension to the chancel.

Ugley has a fine Tudor tower in brick. This is a lovely place, secluded beside a large farm.

Henham is an attractive church in a prime setting, and if this were a competition it would gain big points for its setting. The top of the tower was repaired in brick and the chancel is rendered in a dull grey. Compare it with Helions Bumpstead.

Clavering is very similar to Chrishall and Chishill and like them is heavily crenelated. Although close to old cottages in the centre of the village, it has a large park-like area of land on three sides.

The chancel at Balsham has the unusual feature of clerestory windows and a fine Decorated style east window. The short external stairway in the angle with the south aisle is unusual.

At Hinxton the south porch has been linked to a south aisle. The short Cambridgeshire spire has been likened unkindly to an upturned ice cream cone.

Great Chesterford has been hard done by in the past but is redeemed by the tranquillity of its immense church yard.

Whittlesford, with its south aisle stretching nearly the whole length of the church, is a classic example of a central tower arrangement in a non-cruciform church, sister of Duxford next door.

Elsenham is a Norman church with early narrow windows. It has been repaired with colourful bricks and there is a fine Norman door within the south porch. Its lies secluded outside its 20th century village.

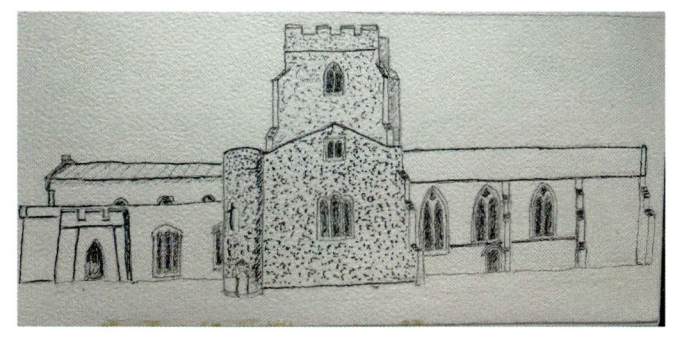

Anstey is a cruciform church with added south aisle. The stairway in the turret at the west corner of the south transept led at one time to an upper floor and the tower.

Linton is a large church with both north and south aisles and porches, and clerestory windows in the nave. It stands secluded down a quiet lane in the middle of this large village.

The Church at Rickling is deep in the countryside a mile from its village. It is a typical Essex Celtic type and its surroundings are notable for the wild flowers.

Anstey is an interesting church, being cruciform, and not least because of the unusual turret on the corner of the south transept.

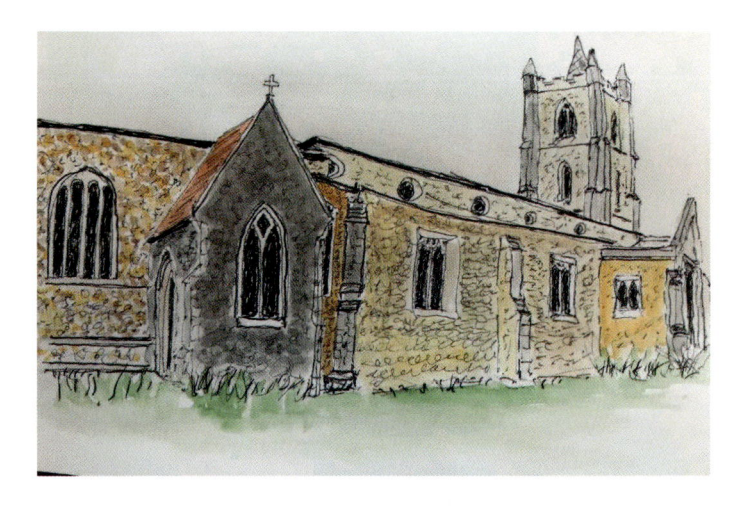

At Little Sampford it is the north side which faces the road and it is this side which has received the most attention over the centuries. The main porch, a north aisle and a small vestry make this the busy side of the church. Notable are the circular clerestory window spaces on the north side of the nave. It is a long church with an unusually low roof line.

Historic England state that there is evidence that construction of the tower was interrupted by the Black Death in 1350.

Away from the village and surrounded by large trees this is an especially lovely place.

Some years before me, Edward Bawden painted this view of the south side of Little Sampford church. Since his time the trees have grown and it has become difficult to get a good view. The only appendage on this side is the 17th century brick porch which is no longer in use. Otherwise it is all 14th century, except for the bright red brick mullions in one window.

Barley received a major restoration by William Butterfield, a well known Victorian architect. Pevsner called the cupola a Butterfield spike.

Helions Bumpstead is remarkable for its clerestory with no north aisle and its range of surfaces and colours.

Wendens Ambo and its Hertfordshire spike. Up the valley Wenden Lofts is named after a landowner, not for its height above the other Wendens..........

............It was closed in 1928: this could happen to a church near you.

The special attraction of small village churches is that they reflect local tastes and ideas. Most of them have oddities of construction where the local mason had his own solutions. Saffron Walden has proved a good centre. There is variety in the surrounding churches and they have much information to impart. Generally age is indicated by the size of the windows; the smaller they are, the older. However that only indicates the age of the window itself, not of the surrounding walls. There are many pitfalls and some Victorians were skilled at imitation.
Throughout the book reference has been made to the mystery of the doors and the different ground plans. Generally there is much to be learned from the less used side of the church. This tends to be the north side, as at Elsenham and Whittlesford, but, as we have seen, some churches have the main door on the north side. In these cases such as Little Sampford, it is the south side which tells more.

They all have the benefit of a quiet churchyard. The best of these are close to the countryside, tranquil, full of birdsong and wild flowers and a little unkempt.

LIST OF CHURCHES INCLUDED

CAMBRIDGESHIRE
Balsham, Bartlow, Castle Camps, Duxford, Great Chishill, Heydon, Hinxton, Ickleton, Linton, Little Abington, Little Chishill, Thriplow, Whittlesford.

ESSEX
Arkesden, Ashdon, Berden, Chickney, Chrishall, Clavering, Debden, Duddenhoe End, Elmdon, Elsenham, Great Chesterford, Hadstock, Helions Bumpstead, Henham, Littlebury, Littlebury Green, Little Bardfield, Little Chesterford, Little Sampford, Newport, Quendon, Radwinter, Rickling, Saffron Walden, Strethall, Thaxted, Ugley, Wenden Lofts, Wendens Ambo, Wimbish.

HERTFORDSHIRE
Anstey, Barley, Meesden